Nicole's World

Living with Down Syndrome

SIMPLICIO PANGILINAN ALBA

ISBN
Hardbound-978-621-8397-95-8
MOBI/KINDLE-978-621-8397-96-5
Softbound/Paperback-978-621-8397-97-2

Published by:
Poetry Planet Book Publishing House
Rosario Pozorrubio, Pangasinan, Philippines
Contact Number: +639554960094
Email: maritesritumalta@gmail.com

WELCOME NOTE

If you are welcoming a new baby into your family or raising a kid with Down Syndrome, you probably have many questions or concerns, as do your extended family, friends, and neighbors.

My daughter Nicole was born with Down syndrome, and I have personally documented some significant life events and milestones for her and gathered some relevant related-stories and facts while keeping in mind my own diverse experiences with her. Nevertheless, the first-hand accounts and collected data discussed here are meant purely for reading enjoyment, reflection, and reference; they should not be used in place of medical advice. Naturally, if your child needs medical assistance, it is still strongly advised that they see a doctor or other health care professional.

May *Nicole's World* be a beacon of hope, showing us the way forward with courage, grace, and unending love. Remember, you are not alone; embrace the journey, the successes, and the beauty that may be found in every step along the way.

DEDICATION

To *Almighty God*, thank you for blessing me with my loving family and for the opportunity to share our story with the world.

To my ever-supportive wife *Rhea*, your steadfast love and understanding have been the anchor that steadies me through life's storms. Thank you for being my partner in life and for nurturing our children with such grace and love.

To my dear son *Joshua*, your unwavering support and kindness have been a source of comfort and strength for our family. Thank you for being the loving and wonderful son and brother that you are.

And to my precious *Nicole*, this book is dedicated to you as a celebration of your spirit and a testament to the beauty and strength that you embody. You have touched our lives in ways we never thought possible, and I am forever grateful for the privilege of being *your father.*

ACKNOWLEDMENT

In the journey of bringing *"Nicole's World: Living with Down Syndrome"* to fruition, I am deeply grateful for the unwavering support and love of my family, whose presence serves as my constant source of strength and inspiration; to my parents, though they have passed on, their words of wisdom and guidance continue to resonate in my heart; and to my siblings and relatives for their unwavering support and encouragement throughout this journey.

To Dr. Goldie and Dr. Arthur Ferrolino, Mrs. Rhina Gube, Mrs. Irene Rogers Cal, and Mrs. Lanyvic Disuanco , I extend my deepest gratitude for giving their consent to include their precious stories in my book. Together with other parents who are blessed with DS children, we journey with love and compassion, embracing the unique beauty and challenges of raising a child with Down Syndrome.

I also wish to acknowledge the invaluable contributions of the experts and researchers on Down Syndrome (special mention to Global Down Syndrome Foundation, Care.com, The Good Schools Guide and N.P. Hamilton) whose tireless efforts have provided answers to my frequently asked questions and served as a vital source of reference.

Lastly, I extend my heartfelt gratitude to Poetry Planet Book Publishing House for providing me with the incredible opportunity to publish "Nicole's World: Living with Down Syndrome." Your belief in the importance of sharing our story and raising awareness about Down Syndrome has been instrumental in bringing this project to fruition.

May God bless us all.

TABLE OF CONTENTS

PART I

Introduction
Flashback
Open Letters
The Creed of Babies with Down Syndrome
Kredo ng Batang may Down Syndrome

Part I

In Part I of this book, let us navigate with you on a heartfelt journey through the days leading up to Nicole's birth, through our eyes, as her family. Here, we describe the emotional rollercoaster of expectation and optimism, from the early fears and worries during her mother's pregnancy to the deep faith in God's providence that kept us going through uncertainty. Alongside this narrative, we also provide the poignant open letters that we, Nicole's parents, and her older brother wrote, which offer an unfiltered look into our feelings and ideas about Nicole's arrival. These letters give a vivid picture of the familial relationship that sustains us through life's difficulties by providing candid insights into the gamut of emotions experienced, from apprehension and fear to boundless love and acceptance.

The anonymously penned *Creed of Babies with Down Syndrome*, which is a potent statement of the intrinsic dignity and worth of individuals with Down Syndrome, has been translated into Filipino as "*Kredo ng Batang may Down Syndrome,*" by the author, this creed echoes the feelings of families affected by Down

Syndrome all throughout the world and embraces the universal values of love, acceptance, and celebration of variety.

We invite readers to journey with us through these insights, bringing empathy, understanding, and everlasting faith in the midst of hardship.

Introduction

It's true, my daughter Nicole is diagnosed with Down Syndrome!

I have to admit that accepting what had transpired was difficult over the first few weeks. My spouse and I had anticipated having one normal, healthy daughter, but we were given a completely different child. There were evenings when I was so distraught by the loss of the daughter I was expecting that I was unable to sleep.

But as the adage states, "Time heals wound as hurt fades away to the point where you can handle it." Now, I can say it gets better.

Indeed, a child is the greatest blessing from God. Whether mentally challenged or not, he/she remains the source of parents' joy and pride. Definitely, when it comes to the bottom line, no parents would want to be put into this boat but since we're in it, we have to love and take good care of our babies.

Hello there! Meet my beautiful daughter

… and welcome to ***Nicole's World***!

Now that you have finally met Nicole, maybe, you're wondering how we have been able to nurture her into a very cheerful, prayerful and loving daughter that she is now. Perhaps, there are numerous questions that you would like to ask me pertaining my daughter's condition, particularly about *Down syndrome related-concerns*.

Allow me then to share with you some real-life stories and observations including my personal experiences in raising my daughter; likewise, share some researches and information from varied sources with the primary aim of making you, my dear readers, gain additional information or insights about Down syndrome and on living with Down syndrome.

Flashback

Although I just kept it to myself, I had a strong feeling that there was a problem with my wife's pregnancy. Seldom did the six-month-old fetus in her belly twitch. Additionally, my wife stated that there were moments when she could hardly feel our baby inside her tummy move.

A child is the greatest blessing from God. Whether mentally challenged or not, he/she remains the source of parents' joy and pride. Thus, we should accept him/her with all our heart no matter what, for what he/she is.

Rhea's "water bag" burst two days prior to giving birth to Nicole, leaking first water and then pure blood. She was rushed to the hospital and, following several hours of monitoring and assessment, was told that the fetus's life within her womb was in danger and that she should have a caesarian section performed right away.

Knowing that Nicole would only have a slim chance of surviving, I gave my heart and thoughts over to God. My wife was taken to the delivery room by the physicians after I had signed the "letter of consent". The procedure worked as planned. Nicole somehow managed to make it. She was told, nevertheless, to move to a different hospital due to her "special" condition. Since there was no ambulance accessible at the moment, I simply rented a doctor's private vehicle. I felt God's presence around me with His mercy and grace as I carried my very frail Nicole, giving her an improvised "oxygen" to help her breathe. Nicole, weighing a just 900 grams, required several weeks to be kept in the incubator. Our school priest performed her baptism within her makeshift nest due to her unsettled state.

It was difficult for me to accept what I had learnt during the first several weeks. There were evenings when I was so distraught by the loss of the daughter I was expecting that I was unable to sleep. Joshua asked me once when his baby sister was coming home. "Dad, when can I see Nicole? Is she still sick? Can you just let her stay here. I promise I'll be a good Kuya to her" . Though anxious, he was eager to see his sister.

His eagerness reminded me of the parent discussing his Down syndrome daughter in the book "Uncommon Fathers". The narrative goes that he was so distraught to learn of his daughter's condition that he chose to have her institutionalized. Their son inquired about his baby sister from him and his wife when they returned home without the baby. They made an effort to clarify the issues around Down syndrome and the reasons his sister would not be returning home. Their son inquired after a short while, "Dad, does this mean that if something happens to me and I'm not so smart anymore, you will also send me away?" When he heard that, they went straight to the institution and brought their child home.

However, unlike the father in the story, I never considered institutionalizing my special child. But just like him, I also felt upset upon learning my daughter's condition. Furthermore, I would most certainly not wait for my son to make the same comments that the boy in the tale had made.

"Son, don't worry. Your younger sister should be home shortly. I said, "Promise me you will love and take good care of Nicole." Joshua smiled and nodded, genuinely saying, "Yes, dad." I swear I will.

Kuya Joshua's Open Letter

Joshua then seven years old wrote:

Hello! I'm Nicole's brother. I frequently questioned my parents about Down syndrome, but I was never able to grasp its whole significance. Nicole is our living angel and a special child; they tell me every time. I do believe them, yes. Nicole is a very precious sister,   definitely.

She can't talk, but I know she recognizes me as her Kuya Josh. She finds a way to play "hide and seek" with me despite her incapacity to walk. She's a hilarious and easygoing playmate.

She might be special because, even at three years old, she still struggles with many basic skills that kids her age can do. However, that does not lessen my affection for her. Even though there are moments when I don't understand her emotions, I always make an effort to be a nice big brother to her by feeding her, helping her with her bath, giving her vitamins, and going to "Early Intervention" therapy sessions with her. Every night, I beg that she could accompany me to school.

Nicole is unique because it is what God made her. I love her no matter what, thus she will always hold a special place in my heart.

Mommy Rhea's Open Letter

February 18, 2001. That was the day that God answered our prayer for a second child. In contrast to my first pregnancy, when I had multiple hospitalizations due to heavy bleeding, I claimed that this one was easier. I even had moments when I didn't believe I was pregnant at all. One thing I did notice, though, was how little the fetus moved inside my womb. I tried not to cry within, even though I was crying all the way up to the day I gave birth to Nicole. She weighed only 900 grams! We also had to move her to another hospital where she was baptized due to her precarious state. She amazingly lived, thank God.

Despite her seeming frailty, she has never before been admitted to the hospital for a serious illness. She has never become a burden to us. She is a happy and kind little girl.

Nicole is unquestionably more than a blessing to our family; in fact, she is our living angel.

Daddy Boyet's Open Letter

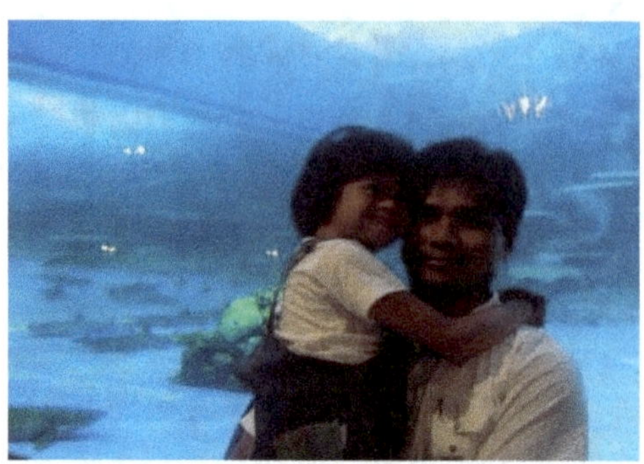

Maybe, Nicole might not have become a teacher like us, her parents, but with love, affection and "early intervention", she would still be able to take care of herself and most importantly, be happy.

It won't be easy to raise a child with Down syndrome, I assure you. However, I genuinely think that if parents know what makes their child resilient and adapts well to having a mentally challenged child, they will see that this is actually a good learning opportunity. Yes, it requires a great deal of labor, but the results are undoubtedly amazing.

Right now, my daughter needs our undying love and support, just like any other child with Down syndrome. I'm aware that she is capable of doing things that all kids can. She might take a little longer, but she will still reach all of the developmental milestones for a young child.

Nicole has improved her performance at a regular school, which is a positive step. With a lot of prayer and perseverance, Nicole can learn to read like any other child and will eventually achieve in her own ways.

The Creed of Babies with Down Syndrome

-Anonymous

My face may be different
But my feelings the same
I laugh and I cry
And I take pride in my gains

        I was sent here among you
        To teach you to love
        As God in the heavens
        Looks down from above

To Him I'm no different
His love knows no bounds
It's those here among you
In cities and towns

        That judge me by standards
        That man has imparted
        But this family I've chosen
        Will help me get started

For I am one of the children
So special and few
That came here to learn
The same lessons as you

That love is acceptance
It must come from the heart
We all have the same purpose
Though not the same start

The Lord gave me life
To live and embrace
And I'll do it as you do
But at my own pace.

Kredo ng Batang may Down Syndrome

(Isinalin sa Tagalog ni Dr. Simplicio Alba)

Maaaring may kakaiba sa aking mukha,
Ngunit pareho lang ang aking nadarama.
Gaya ng aking pag-iyak at pagtawa,
Tulad din ng pamamaraan ng sa iba.

Ipinagmamalaki ko ang aking pinagmulan,
Ako ay ipinadala upang kayo ay turuan.
Sana ako'y paka-ingatan at mahalin,
Dasal sa Diyos, ako sana'y inyong tanggapin.

Sa Kanya hindi ako naiiba,
Binubuhay ako ng pag-ibig Niya.
Ngunit sa paningin ng ibang tao,
Pamantayan nila ay hindi ko gusto.

Subalit ang pamilyang ito na aking pinili,
Tutulong sa aking panimula at tunay na kakandili.

Sapagkat ako na isang munting bata,
Bagamat natatangi at may pagkakaiba.
Dumating dito sa mundo upang alamin,
Parehong aral ng buhay na susuungin.

Na ang pag-ibig ay pagtanggap,
Dapat itong magmula sa puso.
Lahat tayo ay may iisang hangarin,
Bagaman hindi pareho ang tatahakin.

Binigyan ako ng Panginoon ng buhay,
Upang ingatan at yakapin.
Gagawin ko ang anumang bagay,
Sa sariling kakayahan, aking sisikapin.

PART II

LIVING WITH DOWN SYNDROME:

Our Family's Journey

The Part II of this book explores the personal and complex path of our family living with our special daughter, Nicole. We relive the incredible turning points and treasured times we've shared with our wonderful daughter through the lens of our experiences. From her first steps to her distinct outlook on life, we shed light on the bravery and resiliency she exemplifies in facing the world with unwavering resolve. We also examine the close relationship she has with her elder brother, emphasizing the depth of their friendship and the priceless lessons in empathy and understanding it imparts. In the middle of the cultural and personal difficulties we've encountered as parents, we demonstrate the tenacity and courage needed to go past setbacks and appreciate the unique qualities in our daughter.

Our goal as a family is to create a space of unwavering love and acceptance where our daughter is valued for who she is—a source of inspiration and light in our lives. By sharing our story, we wish to encourage others to value uniqueness, accept variety, and discover joy in the remarkable adventure of being a person with Down syndrome.

Nicole and Joshua share a unique bond. She is not just the sister of her older brother, but also her best friend and playmate. There was an instance when they were playing, Nicole had an accident, and she was sobbing uncontrollably that Joshua was at a loss for words to comfort her.

Joshua, then seven years old, enjoyed writing poetry and short stories. He thought that incident would make a wonderful subject for a short narrative.

This is Joshua's account of the events.

Nicole Met an Accident (On Telling the Truth)

(Based on a True Story)
by: CJ Alba, 7 years old

Blaggg!!! "Lola, Nicole fell from the chair," I yelled!

One Monday afternoon, I was playing with my baby sister Nicole. We played together. We were happy laughing. But I left her for a while to urinate. When I was inside our comfort room, I heard a loud cry. I immediately went out of the comfort room to find out what happened. Nicole was crying very loud. Lola Oyang, my mom's aunt, was there so I asked her what had happened. She told me that Nicole went out-of-balance.

"There was a swollen lump on her forehead! Surely, mom and dad will get angry once they know...but should I tell them or not?", I told myself.

When my parents came home from school, Nicole began to cry very loud again.

"What happened to Nicole? Why is she crying?", they asked. With all honesty, I told them everything I knew.

"It was nobody's fault…just an accident," I said.

"Now we understand why she is not feeling well," said my mom.

"I'll get an ice and put it on Nicole's forehead," father said.

Because I told them the truth, my parents were able to think of an immediate remedy. Thank you, God, Nicole became well after an hour and we happily played again.

Summary:

The narrative begins with Nicole falling off a chair while playing and then crying out for help. For a brief period, Joshua is left alone and wonders if he should tell his parents about the accident since he is afraid they might become upset. In the end, he makes the honest decision and tells his parents the truth when they get home. Nicole's injury can be swiftly attended to by Joshua's parents, who appreciate his honesty in getting her the care she requires. Though at first unsettling, Joshua's honest admission results in a happy ending, highlighting the significance of honesty in building trust and promoting efficient communication within the family dynamic.

Guide Questions for Self- Reflection:

1.   What was the effect of Joshua's choice to be honest about Nicole's accident on how things turned out? Reflect on how honesty helped to build trust and made it possible for Joshua's parents to meet Nicole's needs.

____

____

____

____

____

____

____

____

2. How did Joshua's internal conflict over whether or not to tell his parents the truth illustrate how crucial being honest is to forming strong relationships with others? Reflect on how Joshua's honesty improved the relationship with his parents, sister Nicole, and himself, ultimately leading to a positive resolution.

____

____

____

____

____

____

____

____

____

____

Celebrating Nicole's Every Milestone

As parents, we treasure every milestone that Nicole achieves since there are innumerable moments that become ingrained in our hearts during the journey of parenthood. With her distinct charm and tenacity, our Nicole successfully navigates a world where even seemingly easy chores can be difficult. Nicole has a spirit that inspires us every day, whether it's the complex skill of tying her shoes or the seemingly simple act of ascending stairs. Nicole's tenacity is evident despite the obstacles she encounters, such as her little feet that make it difficult for her to move quickly and the dissatisfaction she occasionally experiences when comparing herself to her peers.

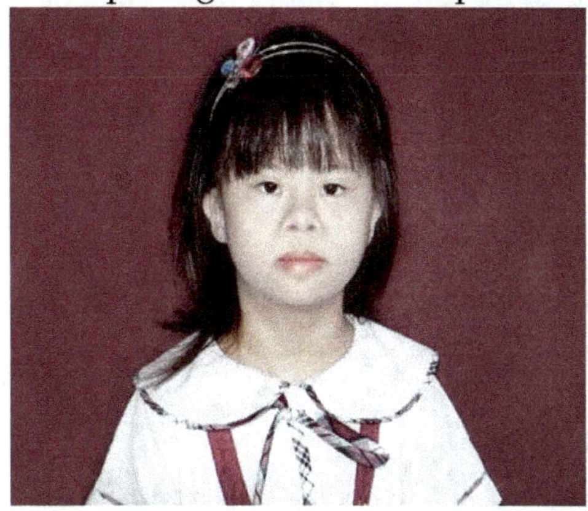

Nicole's journey into mainstream school at five years old was a big deal for all of us. As we saw our little baby take her first steps toward independence, we were overwhelmed with both optimism and anxiety. She began by sitting among her friends, giving them a gentle introduction to the world of learning and socializing. But as time went on, Nicole's self-assurance increased, and before we knew it, she had formally registered as a kindergarten student and was prepared to start a new chapter in her academic career.

Nicole struggles with words, but when she sings, her voice rings out powerful. Her use of music as a language allows her to express herself without being constrained by social norms or other constraints. Nicole has an obvious love for music, whether she's belting out a song or swaying to the beat. Her joy for life's little moments is contagious, and she adores the limelight, unaffected by the stares directed at her.

Nicole sees school as more than simply a place to study; it's a platform where she can also shine. Nicole pursues every opportunity with unrelenting resolve, whether it's taking center stage in events like intramurals or engaging in regular classroom activities. Her willingness to interact with her peers and her inclusive attitude are evidence of her perseverance and of her ability to overcome obstacles with grace.

As parents, we have found it quite amazing to follow Nicole's journey. We have marveled at the depth of her spirit and celebrated her accomplishments, big and little. When it comes to her teacher, Nicole is more than just a student. She is a beacon of kindness and tenacity, and at the end of the school year, her teacher named her the "most behaved pupil"—an honor that makes us incredibly proud.

Guide Questions for Self- Reflection:

1. How do Nicole's achievements, despite the challenges she faces, inspire resilience and perseverance in both herself and those around her? Reflect on the impact of celebrating each milestone, no matter how small, in fostering a sense of accomplishment and empowerment within Nicole and her support system.

____

____

____

---

2. In what ways does Nicole's journey through mainstream schooling exemplify the importance of inclusivity and support in enabling individuals with unique abilities to thrive? Consider the role of educators, peers, and family members in fostering an environment where Nicole feels valued, respected, and capable of achieving her fullest potential.

Embracing Nicole's "Episodes"

Numerous happy moments have interrupted our journey with Nicole, but we also call them "episodes." One particular episode that comes to mind is the celebration of Nicole's eighteenth birthday. Nicole's party, which was being hosted at a resort in Pansol, Laguna, was anticipated with a palpable sense of excitement and her signature ready smile. The food was delicious, the décors were charming, and the mood was joyous. But as the event continued, Nicole's attitude abruptly changed as each guest had a turn speaking and giving her gifts. Tears trickled softly down her cheeks, her previously joyful disposition giving way to a deep melancholy that seemed to come from inside.

At first, we thought Nicole's tears were caused by the intense feelings her visitors' outpouring of love and care had triggered. But as the party went on and it was time for her to dance with her eighteen male guests, it became evident that she was having deeper problems. Her tears and heavy heart betrayed the anguish she was going through on the inside, even though she was making a great effort to participate in the celebrations.

Her abrupt change in behavior alarmed my wife and me as her parents, so we decided to look for information and support to help her through this emotional turmoil.

Nicole temporarily withdrew within herself during the next few days, her melancholy evident at every turn of her face. Determinate to comprehend and manage her emotional fluctuations, we continued her medications, consulted friend-experts and contacted other parents with unusual children who had gone through similar experiences. I threw myself into my studies, reading books and articles from the internet to gain understanding of the particular difficulties that teenagers with Down syndrome encounter.

Alongside Nicole, we set off on a healing journey full of love, tolerance, understanding, and unshakable support. We likewise discovered new locations where she takes pleasure in her favorite pastimes, and find comfort in the great outdoors.

Nicole's soul was lifted by her family's love and dedication, and she gradually emerged from the sadness of her "episode". This difficult experience taught us the priceless lesson that our daughter needs our patience, understanding, and unwavering love to get through her darkest periods. We learned that although obstacles could try our will, they also present chances for development and closer relationships. Above all, we renewed our dedication to walking hand in hand with Nicole and embracing her journey's highs and lows with unshakable love and faith.

Guide Questions for Self- Reflection:

1. How did Nicole's "episode" during her eighteenth birthday celebration serve as a catalyst for deeper reflection on the unique challenges faced by individuals with Down syndrome and their families? Reflect on the complexities of crossing emotional turmoil and the importance of seeking support and understanding from within the community.

____

____

____

____

____

____

____

____

____

____

2. In what ways did Nicole's journey through her "episode" highlight the

transformative power of love, patience, and unwavering support in overcoming adversity? Consider how this experience reinforced the value of embracing vulnerability and facing challenges head-on as a family unit, ultimately strengthening bonds and fostering resilience.

Nicole's Enthusiasm for Life

Nicole's path is characterized by the happiness she finds in each moment rather than only the difficulties she encounters. While some people with Down syndrome experience health issues, Nicole's tenacity comes through as she travels through life largely unaffected. Nicole's heart continues to beat strongly, her vision and hearing are unharmed, and the only condition requiring frequent care is her thyroid—a testament to Nicole's unwavering attitude in the face of hardship.

Nicole loves the small things in life, especially her trips to the mall, which are among of her greatest pleasures. She can indulge in her favorite foods there, savoring the flavor of popcorn and French fries while losing herself in the world of movies. Her taste in food reflects her spirit of adventure; she has a particular fondness for fried chicken, which goes well with "sinangag,".

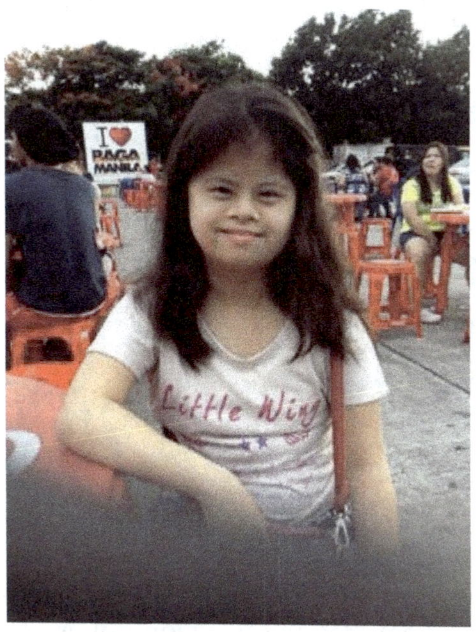

Nicole is enthralled with adventure at every step; it's not simply the flavors of life that appeal to her. Weekends began at the age of seven, when she would go to the mall to ride the thrill-seeking rides, such as the mini-train, carousel, bump cars, and the thrilling "octopus" ride.

Nicole embraces every turn with a captivating zeal that astounds onlookers. She is fearless and full of curiosity.

Nicole's enthusiasm for life, however, knows no bounds to her birthplace. She has crossed boundaries and explored the diverse cultures that lie ahead of her with the help of her devoted family. Nicole has embraced a wide range of experiences, as seen by her passport, which shows her from serene landscapes to busy Asian metropolis. Her travels provide her the chance to make new friends and connections and expand her horizons, which is evidence of her limitless capacity for acceptance and love.

One thing is very evident when we consider Nicole's experience thus far: despite the challenges her condition may cause, it will never define her. She keeps defying expectations day after day, demonstrating that tenacity in the face of adversity, rather than its absence, is what defines strength. And despite everything, our greatest hope for Nicole is still the same: that she will continue to write her tale with unflinching courage and grace, enjoy the beauty of life's small joys, and bask in the warmth of happiness.

Nicole is more than simply a daughter — she is a ray of hope and tenacity. Her story serves as a reminder that resilience may take many different shapes and that overcoming obstacles head-on is the ultimate test of success rather than the absence of obstacles.

We walk this life journey with Nicole, and we do it with hearts full of love and appreciation for the opportunity to be her parents.

Our journey with Nicole as parents has been nothing short of amazing. She came into our life and immediately made our world full of love, laughter, and unending happiness. However, a distinct set of struggles and victories that have molded our family in ways we never could have predicted are also weaved into the tapestry of our tale. The core of the matter is Nicole's diagnosis of Down syndrome, a classification that, despite certain implications, does not define the essence of who Nicole is.

Guide Questions for Self- Reflection:

1. How does Nicole's unwavering enthusiasm for life, despite the challenges she faces, serve as a source of inspiration for those around her? Reflect on how her infectious zest for adventure and exploration encourages others to embrace the beauty and joy found in even the simplest moments of life.

____

____

____

____

____

____

____

____

____

2. In what ways does Nicole's boundless curiosity and love for adventure exemplify the importance of embracing life's opportunities with open arms? Consider how her fearlessness and willingness to explore new experiences not only enrich her own life but also foster a sense of wonder and appreciation in those who have the privilege of journeying alongside her.

____

____

____

____

____

____

____

____

____

Part III

LIVING WITH DOWN SYNDROME:

A Journey of Parents with Down Syndrome Children

LIVING WITH DOWN SYNDROME: *A Journey of Parents with Down Syndrome Children*

The Part III of this book will let us delve into the poignant and meaningful testimonies of parents navigating the unique journey of raising children with Down syndrome. Learn about the many difficulties they have faced through their candid narratives, from the first difficulties accepting their child's diagnosis to the difficulties in offering care and assistance. Yet, amidst the trials , these parents highlight the amazing achievements and delights their unique children have brought into their lives as they tell stories of resiliency, tenacity, and undying love.

Let us embrace the tremendously beneficial influence Down syndrome has had on their families as we immerse ourselves in their varied stories, allow ourselves to be moved by their fortitude, and find comfort in their shared experiences. We are reminded throughout their journey of the beauty inherent in each person's individual journey and the transformational power of love and acceptance.

MY PARENTING JOURNEY WITH DOWN SYNDROME

by *Goldie Majarucon-Ferrolino*

Parenting a child with Down syndrome is a journey best traveled in faith. My own journey is captured by these lyrics from the modern-day hymn, **"God Will Make a Way"** by Don Moen.

"God will make a way when there seems to be no way."

When we got married, I was diagnosed to have PCOS (polycystic ovary syndrome), a common cause of infertility. I was 39 years old then, making it even more difficult for me to conceive because of my age. But God did find a way: After six months of work-up and treatment, I became pregnant with my first child and it was uneventful. I delivered a healthy baby boy by Caesarean section.

My husband and I then prayed for a baby girl to complete our family. God answered our prayer! I became pregnant again with our second child.

"He works in ways we cannot see. He will make a way for me."

This time, it was a difficult pregnancy. On the 29th week of my pregnancy, I delivered a preterm baby girl who only weighed 1.2 kilograms. We named her Anaiah, which in Hebrew means "God answers." Indeed, she was God's answer to our prayers!

God would later reveal to us that prematurity was not the only problem of Anaiah. During her first week in the Neonatal ICU, her pediatrician noticed some features of Down syndrome: upslanted eyes, simian crease on one palm, and slightly protruding tongue. Karyotyping confirmed our worst fear: Anaiah has trisomy 21. Our precious little girl was born with Down syndrome.

"He will be my guide, hold me closely to His side"

Little by little, God revealed to us Anaiah's disabilities and abilities. We found out that she had a congenital heart disease (Atrial septal defect) which did not require heart surgery yet. She started her speech and occupational therapies early and was able to walk independently at age two.

She could do almost all her developmental milestones except for one: We noticed that even at three, she did not babble or follow sounds. Hearing tests confirmed that Anaiah had profound sensorineural hearing loss of both ears. No wonder she would not wake up to the sound of fireworks during New Year. She could not utter simple words like Mama and Papa.

Knowing about Anaiah's impaired hearing once again dampened our spirits, but later, my husband and I learned to accept it by faith and walk with God more closely.

"With love and strength for each new day, He will make a way."

Today, Anaiah is God's work in progress, just like all of us. God continues to work little miracles in her life. She is a budding teenager and currently attends grade 4 in a SPED-inclusive home-based learning school since pandemic. While still not yet able to talk coherently due to her hearing disability, she continues to learn through school and therapies. Every little achievement she has is always a reason to thank and praise God for. Truly, with God, nothing is impossible!

Indeed, parenting a child with Down syndrome is a difficult journey, but it is not a hopeless one. It is not just a walk, but a leap of faith. Faith is not seeing to believe; it is believing first to see that it can be done. And it all starts with fully accepting and embracing God's purpose for your child with Down syndrome.

Your child with Down syndrome is neither an accident nor a punishment nor a burden. He or she is fearfully and wonderfully made by God - a masterpiece to showcase His glory. Accept and embrace God's purpose for your child's life. Develop a heart to follow God, the faith to believe that He is able, and the courage to take that step of faith.

"He will make a way."

Goldie Majarucon-Ferrolino is a medical doctor and has been married for 17 years to Art, also a medical doctor. They are blessed with two beautiful kids, Tristan and Anaiah.

In her insightful parenting journey, Dr. Goldie Majarucon-Ferrolino highlights the value of resilience, acceptance, and faith in raising a kid with Down syndrome. She and her husband were fortunate to become parents to two children, including Anaiah, who was born prematurely and was identified as having Down syndrome, despite early struggles with a challenging pregnancy. They overcame Anaiah's health problems and developmental delays by having faith and tenacity, and they accepted God's plan for her life. Despite obstacles including profound hearing loss and congenital heart condition, Anaiah perseveres, thanks to love, fortitude, and the assistance of medical professionals and educational resources.

Dr. Goldie highlights throughout their journey the significance of accepting and embracing God's purpose for their kid, seeing her as a work of art made to display His glory, and discovering hope and inspiration in the belief that God will make a way.

Guide Questions for Self- Reflection:

1. Reflecting on Dr. Goldie's journey, how does her story challenge your understanding of faith and resilience in the face of unexpected challenges? Consider how her unwavering belief in God's plan and His ability to make a way despite difficulties inspires you to approach your own struggles with greater trust and hope.

---

2. Dr. Goldie emphasizes the importance of accepting and embracing God's purpose for her child with Down syndrome. How does her message encourage you to reevaluate your perspective on disabilities and the value of every individual's life? Reflect on how Dr. Goldie's journey of faith and acceptance prompts you to cultivate a deeper appreciation for diversity and the unique gifts each person possesses, regardless of perceived limitations.

Mrs. Rhina Gube describes her parenting journey with her son, Arjay, 26 years old, who has Down syndrome.

"Si Arjay ay ang anak ko na may Down Syndrome. Panganay siya kaya ng sabihin sa amin na ganoon ang condition niya, 'di agad namin natanggap. 'Acceptance' ang naging problema naming mag-asawa ng sabihin sa amin na may DS nga si Arjay. Kahit lahat na ng signs ay naroon, sinasabi pa rin namin sa sarili namin na normal si Arjay. Naging malaking pagsubok ito para sa amin na magulang kung paano siya palalakihin ng maayos at malusog. Kung paano siya matututo at

maiintindihan ang buhay at ang mga taong nakapaligid sa kaniya."

"Habang si Arjay ay lumalaki na at natututong mag explore, tumatakas siya sa aming bahay at tumatakbo kung saan niya lamang gusto. Nag-aalala kami na baka siya ay hindi makabalik kaya naman dapat ay tutok at bantay talaga, dahil 'pag minsan ay hindi natin alam ang takbo ng isip nila. Kinailangan pa rin na disiplinahin ng maayos para sa kapakanan niya. Ang aking anak ay hindi tuwid magsalita ngunit kaya pa rin niyang i express or ipaintindi kung ano ang gusto niyang sabihin."

"Lahat ng tao na makakakita sa kaniya ay tuwang tuwa dahil si Arjay ay palakaibigan. Kakawayan at ngingitian niya ang mga ito at patatawanin sa pamamagitan ng pagpapa cute at pag sayaw. Si Arjay ngayon ay marunong na sa mga gawaing bahay at siya ay masipag. Kusa siyang kumikilos kapag alam niya na kailangan ng gawin ang isang bagay."

"Hindi ko ikinahihiya na Down Syndrome si Arjay, nagpapasalamat pa po kami dahil wala siyang binibigay na problema sa amin .Naging kasama ko araw araw hanggang sa paglaki nya ay nasa tabi ko lang siya, kumpara sa ibang bata at sa mga binata na may ganitong edad na hindi mo na mahagilap. Parati

akong may baby sa loob ng bahay kahit dalawa na lang kami sa bahay dahil ang Papa niya ay nasa Hongkong at ang kapatid naman niya na mas bata sa kanya ay nasa work na, kaya bihira ng umuuwi dahil tumira na malapit sa work niya sa Paranaque. Nagaaral pa si Arjay sa Pulo National High School kasama niya ang mga special na katulad nya. Masaya siya pag nasa school. Hindi sya nabubully dahil palakaibigan si Arjay lalo na sa kanyang mga guro. Mahilig din siya sa magaganda at meron din siyang damdamin gaya ng sa normal na binata. Yun lang hindi siya naiintindihan sa normal speech niya kasi hindi deretso ang salita niya."

"Sa katulad ni Arjay, mas maswerte sila dahil wala silang problema sa buhay. Happy na si Arjay kung ano ang naibibigay namin sa kanya. Mahilig mangolekta si Arjay ng ring at kwintas, maligaya na siya doon kapag nasa mall kami at mabili lang ng ring, ok na sa kanya. Hindi siya maselan sa mga pagkain, lahat ay kinakain nya, ayaw lang niya ng spicy. Masaya rin si Arjay kapag nanonood ng mga action movies lalo na kapag tungkol Kay Coco Martin at sa Kapamilya Channel gaya ng palabas na ASAP at It's Showtime. Maligaya na siya kapag may YouTube, dahil mahilig siyang kumanta at sumayaw. Naranasan na ni Arjay ang sumakay ng eroplano , ferry boat nakapunta na siya sa Hongkong ,Disneyland, Ocean Park, Macau, Boracay, at marami pang iba."

"Mahirap nung una ngunit masaya ang naging buhay ng aming pamilya nang dahil kay Arjay. Siya ang nagbibigay ng pag-asa sa aming araw araw. Siya ay malaking biyaya sa amin at aming ipagmamalaki. Kami ay nagpapasalamat dahil siya ay binigay sa aming pamilya."

"Sa ngayon ay may alaga kaming puppy at libangan na rin po ni Arjay na makipaglaro sa puppy niya."

The story centers on Arjay, Mrs. Rhina Gube's son who has Down syndrome, and it depicts the process of acceptance, difficulties, and joys that come with raising him. After initially finding it difficult to accept Arjay's condition in spite of clear indications, the parents go through a difficult trial to learn how to raise him in a way that is both fulfilling and healthy. As Arjay gets older, his curiosity raises questions about his safety, but his outgoing personality and eagerness to interact with people make people happy. Arjay finds it difficult to communicate verbally, but his capacity for understanding and self-expression is acknowledged, and he takes an active part in domestic tasks and enjoys school because of his friends and teachers. Despite popular belief,

Arjay's modest pleasures and tenacity—exhibited by his passion for collecting objects and his appreciation of entertainment—bring him great satisfaction. His family is appreciative of his presence and the optimism he gives them.

The significance of love, acceptance, and thankfulness in overcoming the challenges of parenting a kid with Down syndrome is shown by Arjay's story. Despite early difficulties, Arjay's presence brings the family great joy and contentment, and they learn to value his special gifts and contributions to their lives. Arjay's travel, hobby, and relationship experiences highlight the richness of his life and his family's dedication to giving him love and support. In the end, Arjay's story offers hope and serves as a reminder of the benefits of accepting variety and appreciating each person's individuality, regardless of their skills or apparent limits.

Guide Questions for Self- Reflection:

1. How does Arjay's story challenge your perceptions and understanding of individuals with Down syndrome and

disabilities in general? Reflect on the journey of acceptance, difficulties, and joys portrayed in the narrative, and consider how it prompts you to reevaluate your attitudes towards diversity, inclusion, and the value of every individual's unique contribution.

____

____

____

____

____

____

____

____

____

____

____

2. In what ways does Arjay's story inspire you to reflect on the importance of love, acceptance, and gratitude in navigating life's challenges and uncertainties? Reflect on the family's journey of learning to embrace Arjay's condition, finding joy in his presence, and

appreciating the simple pleasures and resilience he embodies, and consider how this resonates with your own experiences of overcoming adversity and finding meaning and fulfillment in unexpected places.

Mrs. Irene Rogers Cal narrates her parenting journey with her beloved daughter, Yehan, 13 years old, who has Down syndrome.

"Noong 3 years old pa lang siya, ipinasok na namin siya sa special education school. Gusto kasi namin na ituring siyang isang normal na bata kahit maraming limitasyon sa kanyang pagkatuto. May mga health problems din siyang hinarap. Naalala ko noong 8 years old pa lang siya, nahihirapan siyang mag "poo-poo". May concern din siya sa kanyang "thyroid". Naagapan naman iyon kasi nagpa-assess kami sa specialist at nabigyan siya ng mga gamot."

"May mga pagkakataon na nalulungkot ako dahil sa ibang mga taong hindi nakakaunawa ng

kanyang kondisyon. Minsan pa nga may nagtanong sa akin kung bakit daw ako nagkaroon ng anak na may Down Syndrome. Naitatanong ko din naman iyan sa sarili ko na kung bakit binigyan ako ni God ng espesyal na anak, pero alam ko may dahilan si God."

"Masipag at masiyahin si Yehan. Nauutusan na namin siya sa gawaing bahay. Madalas pa nga, nagkukusa na siyang maglinis ng bahay, maghugas ng plato, magcheck kung sarado ang pinto, ang bintana o ang gasul. Hindi siya mahiyaing bata. Kinagigiliwan siya kasi palagi siyang naka-smile. Sa school, sumasali siya sa activities. Kaya niyang sumayaw at kumanta."

"Simple lang ang pangarap ni Yehan. Nabanggit niya sa akin na gusto niyang bumili ng

bahay para sa akin at magkaroon ng cellphone. Kaya naman gagalingan niya daw sa pagba-blog. Madasalin si Yehan. Siya ang nagli-lead ng prayer bago kami kumain at bago matulog. Minsan nga nabanggit niya sa akin na tinatanong daw siya ni God kung sino ang gusto niyang maging magulang. Ang sabi daw niya kay God ay sina Irene at Jason lang.

Mahal na mahal namin si Yehan. Lagi ko ngang sinasabi sa kanya na mahal ko siya habang buhay, na kapag nawala siya, sasabay na ako. "

The conducted interview with her mother depicts Yehan's (a child with Down syndrome) journey through her struggles and triumphs. Yehan's parents enroll her in a special education school and seek medical attention for her, when necessary, in an effort to provide her a normal upbringing, despite her academic disabilities and health issues, including thyroid and "poo-poo" problems.

They struggle with misconceptions in society and wonder why they had a kid with Down syndrome, but they take comfort in the idea that God has a purpose. Yehan is shown as being loved by her family, prayerful, happy, and hardworking. She takes an enthusiastic interest in both school activities and household responsibilities. Her simple dreams, like owning a cellphone and purchasing a house for her parents, demonstrate her optimism and determination, while her close relationship with her parents is evident in their expressions of unconditional love and support.

Guide Questions for Self- Reflection:

1. How does Yehan's story challenge your perceptions and understanding of individuals with Down Syndrome? Reflect on the struggles and triumphs Yehan faces, particularly in terms of education, health, and societal attitudes, and

consider how this impacts your perspective on inclusivity and empathy towards individuals with disabilities.

____

____

____

____

____

____

____

____

____

____

2. In what ways does Yehan's story inspire you to reconsider your own assumptions about happiness, success, and fulfillment? Reflect on Yehan's resilience, determination, and simple dreams, despite the challenges she encounters, and consider how her story encourages you to appreciate the small joys in life, embrace diversity, and prioritize love and acceptance in your own relationships and aspirations.

75

Mrs. Lanyvic Disuanco narrates her parenting journey with her beloved daughter, Chelsea Joy, 18 years old, who has Down syndrome.

"Si Chelsea ay ipinanganak ko na may Down syndrome via caesarian section. Noong una, ang hirap tanggapin at napakaraming tanong sa isip namin, kung bakit. Nandoon din iyong big question kung bakit naman, Lord. Pero after one week, nag-usap kami ng masinsinan ng asawa ko at buong puso naming tinanggap si Chelsea dahil siya ay anak namin at siya ay ipinagkaloob sa amin ng Panginoon. At ang ibig sabihin ay kaya namin."

"Akala namin ay doon na natatapos ang problema, madami pa palang parating na pagsubok para sa aming mag-asawa. Noong 5 months old na si Chelsea ay na-diagnose na may dalawang butas siya sa puso, at ang kanyang development ay globally-delayed. Tinapat kami ng doctor na kailangan siyang maoperahan sa puso as soon as possible kasi ay hindi daw magsasara ng kusa 'yung butas sa puso niya. Dalawa kasi ang butas at malalaki pa. Tinapat din kami ng doctor na kung hindi namin siya mapaopera ay hanggang 3 years old lang daw ang life span niya".

"That time, sobrang gumuho ang mundo naming mag-asawa dahil kakaumpisa lang namin at walang-wala din kami sa mga panahon na 'yun. Sobrang mahal magpaopera lalo na sa puso at may anak pa kami na 3 years old, 'yung sinundan ni Chelsea. Mula noong 5 months old siya, kada buwan 2-3 times kaming naka-confine sa hospital dahil nga siya ay may congenital heart problem at nati-trigger din yung lungs niya. Hanggang sa umabot na kami sa point at tinapat ng doctor na umuwi na lang kami. Magsign na lang ng waiver dahil hindi na tinatanggap ng katawan ni Chelsea ang mga gamot,

at kung makikita niyo lang siya that time ay sobrang maaawa at maiiyak kayo kasi bedridden siya at sobrang malnuorished ,halos butot-balat, halos kita na 'yung skull niya sa sobrang nipis ng balat."

"So ayun na nga, wala kaming nagawa kundi umuwi at pagdating namin sa bahay ay hindi ko na alam ang gagawin ko. Ang hirap at sakit sa dibdib na nakikita mo ang anak mo na naghihirap at halos minu-minuto ay nadumi siya ng dugo. Sa sobrang desperada ko na mabuhay lang anak ko ay nagkulong ako sa kwarto at nagdasal ng sobrang taimtim sa Panginoon. Masasabi ko na 'yung tipong nasa harapan ko ang Panginoon at nakipag bargain sa kanya na kung gusto niyang kunin si Chelsea ay kunin na niya kasi sobrang hirap na ang anak ko. Kung hindi naman, ipahiram niya ng habang buhay sa amin si Chelsea at ipinapangako ko na aalagaan namin siya ng buong puso.

"Nagdasal din ako na bigyan niya ako ng sign kung paano matigil ang pagdumi niya ng dugo ng sunod-sunod. Habang ako'y nagdadasal bigla na lang sumagi sa isip ko 'yung bote ng gamot (reseta ng doctor) na nasa maleta namin na halos 6 months na nakatambak at wala ng laman. Binili namin 'yun nung inuwi ko si Chelsea at pinacheck sa pediatrician *sa Davao. Inuwi ko siya doon para dalhin sa mga faith healer. Laking Davao kasi ako kaya naniniwala sa mga hilot at manggagamot. Kasi kapag magulang ka, lahat ay gagawin mo, susubukan mo, para lang sa anak mo."*

"Purihin ang Panginoon, kapag pala ikaw ay nagdasal ng buong puso at lahat ay isinurrender mo na ayon sa kagustuhan niya ay wala pala talagang imposible sa Panginoon. To cut the story short, tumigil ang pagdumi ni Chelsea ng dugo at hindi ko rin mawari o maisip kung bakit sumagi din sa isip ko na itigil na lahat ng gamot ni Chelsea. Ang

tanging iniwan ko lang at ipinapainom sa kanya ay 'yung paper tab para sa puso niya, the rest na mga gamot ay itinapon ko. At hindi ko itinigil ang pagpa-breast feed sa kanya that time kahit 2 years and 3 months old na siya, kasi sabi ng doctor ay mas nakakatulong ang gatas ng nanay lalo na sa case ni Chelsea. That time tinatiyaga naming painumin ng gatas na naka baso at kutsara si Chelsea, iyon ang gamit para mainon niya kasi hindi siya nadede sa bote kundi nasanay kasi sa akin. Gumagawa din ako ng mixed vegetables, na nilalaga at biniblender at iyon ang ipinapakain sa kanya."

"Sa awa ng Diyos at pagtitiyaga namin, si Chelsea ay nagkalaman at nag-uumpisang mag gabay-gabay at maglakad. Sobrang miracle talaga ang naranasan namin that time at salamat sa Panginoon buhay. At nung si Chelsea ay 2 years and 11 months old na, siya ay pina andioplasty namin para malaman kung pwede pa ba siyang maoperahan. Sa awa ng Diyos ay pwede pa. Kasi kung napatagal-tagal pa daw ng ilang buwan ay hindi na siya pwedeng operahan sabi ng doctor. Ang ginawa kay Chelsea ay total correction open heart surgery at after 2 months mula ng maoperahan siya *ay sobrang nagtuloy-tuloy na ang paggaling ni Chelsea, as in wala ng bawal, wala ng gamot kahit ano. Pwede na niyang gawin lahat, kaya sobrang thank you, Lord talaga kasi hanggang ngayon ay malusog at masayahin ang aming Chelsea."*

"Ang aming mahal na si Chelsea ay 18 years old na ngayon. Siya ay super active at nag-aaral pa din sa secondary special education at the same time, nagpa-partime model. And looking forward to work at Shakey's soon. Walang mga pagsubok na hindi natin nalalagpasan at walang ibinibigay ang

Panginoon na hindi natin kaya. God is good all the time. Manalig ka lang at ikaw ay pakikinggan. Amen."

Mrs. Lanyvic Disuanco recounts the difficulties they had when Chelsea was diagnosed with two holes in her heart at the age of five months, as well as the first difficulty they had accepting her daughter's diagnosis of Down syndrome. Even though they were facing an enormous emotional and financial hardship, they decided to take a leap of faith and prayed a lot for Chelsea to survive. In a moment of desperation, Chelsea's mother prayed and stopped taking unneeded medications, which caused a miraculous turn of events to occur. Chelsea overcome her health issues, had a successful heart surgery, and started to thrive—defying the doctor's initial prediction that she would not live long—thanks to God's kindness and their unwavering patience. Chelsea, at eighteen, is a dynamic young woman who is thriving academically, actively seeking modeling possibilities, and looking forward to her future initiatives. She is a living example of the family's tenacity and the ability of faith to overcome seemingly insurmountable challenges.

The testimony of Mrs. Lanyvic is a moving reminder of the unending strength that comes from submitting to God's will and having faith in His plan—even in the face of unfathomable difficulties. Her experience encourages contemplation on the transforming potential of faith, tenacity, and parental love by showing that, with God's grace, no hardship is insurmountable and no barrier is too great to be overcome. Chelsea's family's journey allowed them to personally witness the amazing effects of divine intervention, which strengthened their unwavering faith in God's goodness and capacity to lead them through the most trying times in life.

Guide Questions for Self- Reflection:

1. Reflecting on Mrs. Disuanco's journey, how does her story of acceptance, desperation, and eventual miracle challenge your understanding of faith and perseverance in the face of adversity? Consider how her unwavering trust in God's plan and her determination to seek solutions for Chelsea's health issues inspire you to

approach your own challenges with greater resilience and reliance on faith.

---

2. Chelsea's mother emphasizes the importance of surrendering to God's will and trusting in His power to overcome obstacles. How does her narrative encourage you to reevaluate your own perceptions of hope and resilience? Reflect on how her experience of witnessing Chelsea's recovery through prayer and perseverance prompts you to cultivate a deeper sense of trust in divine

intervention and the strength to navigate life's challenges with unwavering faith.

PART IV

Frequently Asked Questions about Down Syndrome

Frequently Asked Questions about Down Syndrome

We frequently find ourselves looking to the wealth of information and experience provided by researchers and subject matter experts in our quest to comprehend and negotiate the difficulties of Down syndrome. What exactly is Down syndrome, and what qualities make it what it is? These are very scientific and medically profound questions that go well beyond the purview of personal experience. Experts have shed light on the distinct problems and strengths that people with Down syndrome possess by delving into the complexities of this genetic disorder through painstaking research and the knowledge gained from years of observation.

As parents, we have a great duty, one that requires us to do more than just love and support our kids; we also have to equip ourselves with the information and tools needed to give them the best care possible. We rely on the knowledge of experts to help us on this journey, from comprehending the early warning signs and symptoms of Down syndrome to investigating the numerous therapies and educational opportunities available. We become more aware of our child's needs and talents with each question we ask and response we look for, which gives us the ability to stand up for their rights and encourage their potential.

 ### *What is Down syndrome?*

Perhaps many of you are not yet aware of the following compiled information regarding Down syndrome, which was shared by Hamilton (2022) and the Global Down Syndrome Foundation (2024):

> ➢ Down syndrome is named after the English physician John Langdon Down, who was the first to categorize the common features of people with the condition.

> ➢ There is no connection between Down syndrome and factors like race, nationality, religion, or anything the

mother or father did before becoming pregnant.

➤ The cause of Down syndrome is unknown. The two copies of chromosome 21 fail to split apart during egg formation in a process known as non-disjunction, resulting in an egg with two copies of the chromosome. After fertilization, this egg produces a baby that has three copies of chromosome 21 in each of its cells. This non-disjunction's reason is still a mystery.

➤ Although individuals with Down syndrome experience physical and cognitive delays from birth, the population as a whole possesses a wide range of abilities that are impossible to predict ahead of time.

➤ For infants with Down syndrome, early intervention is crucial. For a child's first five years of life, receiving the proper speech and physical therapy can have a significant impact on their intellectual and physical development.

➢ It's critical that people and children with Down syndrome receive the appropriate medical treatment. It can have a significant impact on the individual's growth, both mentally and physically.

➢ Despite having certain characteristics in common, individuals with Down syndrome tend to resemble their immediate family members rather than one another.

➢ Typical but not universal characteristics include small height, a round face, almond-shaped and an up-slanting eyes. These characteristics are not medical conditions.

➢ Although no one knows for sure why Down syndrome occurs and the chromosomal error that causes it cannot be prevented, scientists have determined that women 35 years of age and above have a markedly increased chance of bearing a kid who has the condition. For instance, a woman's chances of conceiving a child with Down syndrome are roughly 1 in 1,000 at age 30. By the age of 35, those odds rise to roughly 1 in 400. Around 40, the risk increases to roughly 1 in 100.

Guide Questions for Self- Reflection:

1. How can parents navigate the initial emotions and uncertainties upon learning that their child has Down syndrome, considering the wide range of abilities and potential outcomes for individuals with this condition?

____

____

____

____

____

____

____

____

____

____

____

Points to ponder:

- Reflect on how your perceptions of disability may influence your initial reactions.

- Consider seeking support from medical professionals, support groups, and other parents of children with Down syndrome.

- Explore your expectations and hopes for your child's future while remaining open to embracing their unique journey.

2. What steps can parents take during their child's early years to ensure optimal development and well-being, understanding the importance of early intervention and specialized therapies?

____

____

____

____

____

____

____

____

____

Points to ponder:

- Reflect on the significance of early speech and physical therapy in fostering your child's intellectual and physical growth.

- Consider the challenges and opportunities involved in advocating for your child's needs within the healthcare system and educational institutions.

- Explore strategies for creating a nurturing and inclusive environment at home that promotes your child's independence and self-esteem.

3. How can parents cultivate a supportive and empowering relationship with their child with Down syndrome, recognizing the importance of medical treatment, while embracing their individuality and unique family traits?

____

____

____

____

____

____

____

____

____

Points to ponder:

- Reflect on the impact of medical treatment on your child's overall well-being and development.

- Consider how to balance the need for medical interventions with fostering a sense of autonomy and self-acceptance in your child.

- Explore ways to celebrate and embrace your child's identity, while also acknowledging the influence of family traits and characteristics.

Characteristics/ Physical Features of Down Syndrome

As a parent who is closely observing my daughter's physical attributes and conversing with other parents of kids who have Down syndrome, I have noticed remarkable similarities in their distinct features. Consulting various references has confirmed that these features are commonly associated with Down syndrome and are indeed present in my daughter.

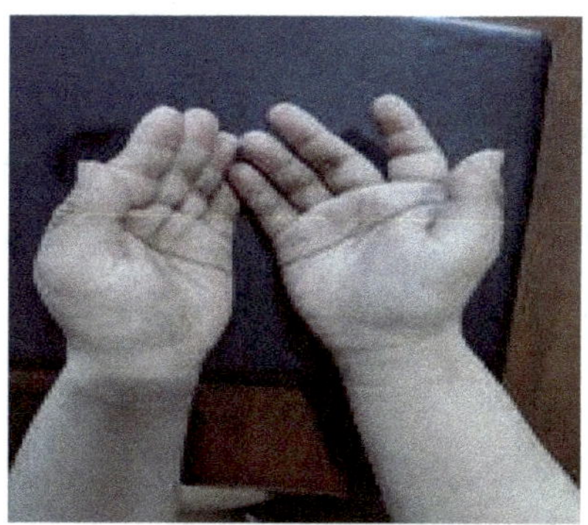

Nicole has wide feet with short toes, and the distance between her big toe and the other toes is wider than usual. Her ears have a little curled top and are smaller. Her head has her ears positioned slightly lower.

Nicole has flat, wide hands with short fingers that tilt inward at the little finger. Her palms have a Simian line. It is referred to as the "Simian crease" or "Single transverse palmar crease" in medicine, and it is usually another indicator of Down syndrome.

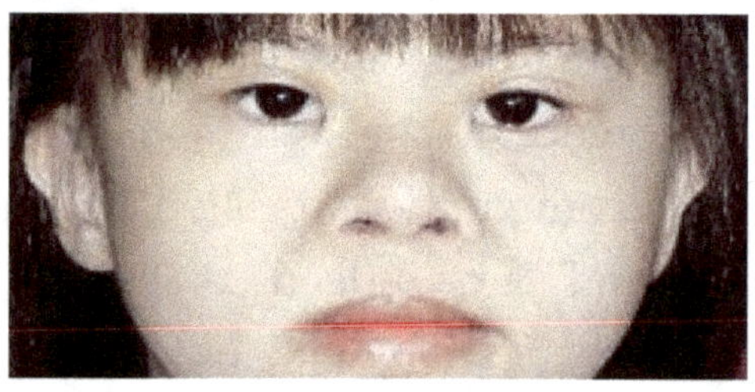

Her eyeballs are tilted upward and outward. There is a fold of skin on the inner side of her eye (epicanthal fold). She has a short, narrow eye slit.

Nicole's mouth is a little bit small and her lips are thin which sometimes leads to her tongue sticking out because the inside of her mouth is smaller.

However, contrary to what the majority of studies claimed, not every person with Down syndrome possesses every one of these traits.

Thus, it's critical to keep in mind that people with Down syndrome are more like their family than they are like one other.

 ***How can a parent adjust to having a child with Down syndrome?***

It's completely normal for parents of children with Down syndrome to experience a difficult transition when they learn about their child's special needs. For me, acceptance and unconditional love have been essential in changing my perspective and goals for my daughter. As Nicole has developed into a sweet and loving child, my wife and I have learned to embrace both her strengths and weaknesses.

We celebrate every milestone she reaches and offer support through every obstacle she encounters. Nicole's doctor visits help us stay proactive about her health. Although Nicole takes her time finishing tasks, we concentrate on her progress rather than comparing her to other children her age, all in an effort to help her reach her full potential.

We also consult medical experts when we have concerns about her health and adjust therapy and educational plans to meet her requirements. Additionally, sharing experiences and coping mechanisms with other parents in similar circumstances through support groups has been a tremendous help and source of moral support.

Guide Questions for Self- Reflection:

1. How can parents navigate the process of grieving the loss of the envisioned future they had for their child, and begin embracing new dreams and aspirations that are tailored to their child's unique abilities and potential?

____

____

____

____

____

____

____

____

____

____

Points to ponder:

- Reflect on the emotions and challenges associated with letting go of preconceived expectations and adjusting to the reality of raising a child with Down syndrome.

- Consider how embracing new dreams and goals for your child can foster resilience and acceptance within your family.

- Explore strategies for finding hope and purpose in supporting your child's growth and development, while honoring their individuality and strengths.

2. What steps can parents take to cultivate a balanced perspective on their child's abilities and challenges, recognizing and

celebrating their strengths while addressing their areas of need?

____

____

____

____

____

____

____

____

____

Points to ponder:

- Reflect on the importance of acknowledging and accepting your child's unique capabilities and limitations.

- Consider the impact of refraining from comparisons with other children and instead focusing on your child's progress and achievements.

- Explore ways to foster a positive and supportive environment at home that promotes self-esteem and confidence in your child.

3. How can parents build a comprehensive support network to address their child's health, emotional well-being, and educational needs, while also prioritizing their own self-care and emotional resilience?

____

____

____

____

____

____

____

____

____

Points to ponder:

- Reflect on the value of seeking support from healthcare professionals, therapists, and other parents who have experience raising children with Down syndrome.

- Consider the importance of designing a personalized therapeutic and educational program that meets your child's specific needs and promotes their overall development.

- Explore strategies for managing stress, seeking emotional support, and finding moments of joy and fulfillment in the journey of parenting a child with Down syndrome.

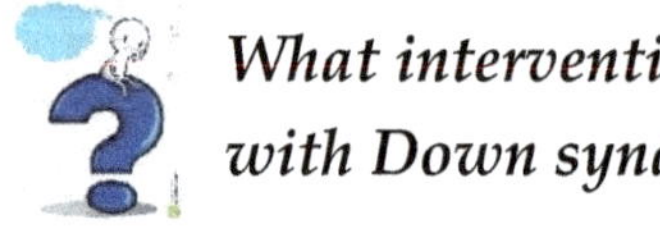

What interventions have helped kids with Down syndrome?

From a personal standpoint, raising my daughter Nicole, who has Down syndrome, has been a life-changing experience full of happiness and progress. Enrolling her in prekindergarten and early intervention programs was one of the most important decisions we made, as it greatly aided in the development of her motor, linguistic, and social abilities.

Nicole's weekly physical therapy sessions were very helpful in promoting her developmental progress. Her muscle tone and coordination improved as a result of these lessons, and she also gained the confidence to accomplish milestones like sitting up, turning over, and eventually speaking confidently.

Occupational therapy played a crucial role in helping Nicole improve her speech, hand-eye coordination, feeding abilities, and social skills as she became older. Her unique demands were met by occupational therapy's customized approach, which helped her become more independent in navigating the outside world.

For Nicole, moving to a conventional preschool was a big accomplishment. It was very helpful for her to interact with her peers in a diverse learning environment. Nicole thrived via play and interacting with other kids, picking up important knowledge and abilities to go along with her official schooling.

Nicole developed a passion for dancing, which gave her substantial advantages for her physical and mental health in addition to enjoyment. Dancing was therapy in the form of balance and confidence-building for Nicole, whether she was learning complex moves or flowing elegantly to the beat.

With regard to dancing, Nicole can compete even with the best dancers in class. She has ears for music

thus she knows proper timing and can easily memorize dance steps.

I added one-on-one tutoring sessions to Nicole's schooling, utilizing my experience as a teacher. We were able to meet her unique learning style and interests thanks to this individualized approach, which improved both her academic and cognitive growth.

Nicole's involvement in school activities was an additional factor that enhanced her overall experience. She flourished in the encouraging environment of her school, making deep connections with both her instructors and classmates through participatory activities and creative arts.

Upon reflection, Nicole's holistic development has been nurtured by the combination of early intervention programs, specialized therapy, and social engagement opportunities. Every intervention has had a distinct impact on her ability to realize her full potential and meet obstacles head-on with tenacity and resolve.

Guide Questions for Self- Reflection:

1. How can parents identify and prioritize interventions that address the specific developmental needs and strengths of their child with Down syndrome, considering factors such as motor skills, language acquisition, socialization, and overall well-being?

____

____

____

____

____

____

____

____

____

Points to ponder:

- Reflect on the effectiveness of various interventions, such as physical therapy, occupational therapy, speech therapy, and hippotherapy, in promoting your child's physical and cognitive development.

- Consider the importance of tailoring interventions to meet your child's individual needs and preferences, while also considering their age, interests, and stage of development.

- Explore strategies for incorporating a combination of interventions into your child's daily routine, while also allowing flexibility to adapt based on their progress and changing needs.

2. How do parents navigate the decision-making process regarding the continuation or discontinuation of specific interventions, such as speech therapy or physical therapy, as their child progresses through different stages of development and transitions into new environments, such as preschool or dance classes?

____

____

____

____

____

____

____

____

____

____

Points to ponder:

- Reflect on the criteria used to evaluate the effectiveness of interventions and determine whether they are still beneficial for your child's growth and development.

- Consider the importance of monitoring your child's progress and consulting with healthcare professionals, educators, and therapists to make informed decisions about ongoing interventions.

- Explore the impact of balancing intervention therapies with other activities, such as socializing with peers, participating in extracurricular activities, and pursuing interests that contribute to your child's overall well-being and happiness.

3. How can parents foster a holistic approach to supporting their child's development, incorporating a variety of interventions, activities, and experiences that promote physical, cognitive, social, and emotional growth?

____

____

____

____

____

____

____

____

____

Points to ponder:

- Reflect on the role of alternative therapies, such as hippotherapy and dance classes, in enhancing your child's physical fitness, coordination, and socialization skills.

- Consider the importance of providing opportunities for your child to explore different interests and hobbies that contribute to their overall development and sense of identity.

- Explore strategies for advocating for inclusive environments and resources that support your child's participation in various activities and promote their inclusion in the community.

What is the parent role in dealing with the Early Intervention system?

As parents, we are reminded that when we find out our child has Down syndrome, we instantly become their strongest advocate. Despite feeling unfamiliar with this role, we soon learn how important it is to actively participate in our child's care and development. In addition to figuring out the intricacies of Down syndrome and maybe becoming parents for the first time, we also find ourselves having to learn how to select and advocate for the best services tailored to our child's needs.

It's important to understand that, even though we may consult with a variety of specialists, we, as parents, are in the best position to decide which services will be most beneficial to our child. We have the authority to decide how best to assist and care for them. Knowing that we have the freedom to make adjustments as needed if we find an Early Intervention program that better meets our child's requirements is empowering.

Here are some useful suggestions/recommendations from Care.com (2024) and from conducted interviews with parents who have children with Down syndrome to help us streamline our advocacy efforts: First, make sure we have the therapist's notes at the conclusion of each treatment session and make copies for our records. These notes are really helpful in monitoring our child's development and assessing how well the therapy is working. It's also helpful to document all of the questions we ask the therapist and the responses we receive. It's critical that we communicate clearly with the therapist, and we should feel free to ask any questions that come up. The therapist's primary role is to support our family; thus, we should anticipate honest and transparent communication from them at all times.

Guide Questions for Self- Reflection:

1. How does recognizing your role as your child's primary advocate within the Early Intervention system influence your approach to seeking and evaluating services for your child with Down syndrome?

Points to ponder:

- Reflect on the shift in perspective from being a passive recipient of services to actively advocating for your child's needs and rights within the Early Intervention system.

- Consider the importance of being informed and empowered to make decisions about the services that best support your child's development and well-being.

- Explore how your unique insights into your child's strengths, preferences, and challenges position you as the most qualified judge of which services are most beneficial for them.

2. How can parents effectively utilize documentation and communication strategies to navigate the Early Intervention system, ensuring that their child receives appropriate services and support?

____

____

____

____

____

____

____

____

____

____

Points to ponder:

- Reflect on the significance of maintaining detailed records of therapy sessions and interactions with therapists, including notes and questions asked.

- Consider how organized record-keeping can facilitate ongoing assessment of your child's progress and inform decisions about the effectiveness of interventions.

- Explore strategies for fostering clear and open communication with therapists, advocating for transparency and accountability in the delivery of Early Intervention services.

3. How can parents cultivate a collaborative and respectful partnership with therapists and service providers within the Early Intervention system, while also asserting their authority and advocating for their child's best interests?

____

____

____

____

____

____

____

____

____

____

Points to ponder:

- Reflect on the importance of building trust and mutual respect with therapists, recognizing their expertise while also asserting your role as the primary decision-maker for your child.

- Consider how effective communication, active listening, and shared goal-setting can strengthen the collaborative relationship between parents and therapists.

- Explore strategies for advocating for your child's needs and preferences within the Early Intervention system, including the option to switch to alternative programs, if necessary, while also fostering a supportive and cooperative partnership with service providers

 ***Can a child with Down syndrome go to school?***

Without a doubt, yes. A child who has Down syndrome can go to school. The good news is that, beginning in preschool, there are specialized programs available to help children with Down syndrome develop their skills to the greatest extent possible. Take Nicole, for example. At just 5 years old, she began her educational journey in a preschool setting, initially as an observer. Her psychomotor skills and socialization have begun to improve despite her cognitive difficulties. Many thanks to her school, which welcomed her and handled her with the same respect as any other student who was enrolled regularly.

This inclusive approach isn't just beneficial for Nicole; it's a model that many children with Down syndrome can benefit from. By blending specialized education with integration into standard classrooms, these children now have a considerably better future ahead of them. Along with learning to read and write, they can also actively participate in various activities both in school and in their communities.

As these children grow into teenagers and eventually adults, opportunities continue to open up. Many persons with Down syndrome are now able to work in traditional employment, despite the fact that there are work programs specifically designed for them. I am aware of numerous positive accounts of teenagers with Down syndrome who are now employed as professional models, entrepreneurs, crew members, product endorsers, etc. A rising percentage of adult people with Down syndrome now lead semi-independent lives in communities.

Based on conducted researches and the accounts of other parents whose teens have Down syndrome, there are now some adults with Down Syndrome who currently choose to live in community group homes in semi-independent settings. Here, they get skills in self-care, helping out around the house, making friends, and engaging in leisure activities—all while becoming engaged citizens of their communities.

The opportunities for people with Down syndrome are growing thanks to inclusive surroundings, education, and support, opening doors to a future full of possibilities.

Guide Questions for Self- Reflection:

1. How does understanding the availability of special programs and support services for children with Down syndrome shape your perspective on their potential for attending school and participating in educational opportunities?

____

____

____

____

____

____

____

____

____

____

Points to ponder:

- Reflect on the significance of early intervention and special education programs in helping children with Down syndrome develop their skills and reach their full potential.

- Consider the impact of inclusive education practices and partial integration into standard classroom settings on promoting socialization, academic growth, and overall well-being for children with Down syndrome.

- Explore the role of schools and educational institutions in creating inclusive environments that support the diverse needs of students with Down syndrome and foster their academic and personal development.

2. How can parents and educators collaborate to ensure that children with Down syndrome receive appropriate support and accommodations to thrive in school settings, while also fostering their independence and self-determination?

____

____

____

____

____

____

____

____

____

____

Points to ponder:

- Reflect on the importance of advocating for individualized education plans (IEPs) and accommodations that address the unique strengths, challenges, and learning styles of children with Down syndrome.

- Consider the role of teamwork and communication between parents, educators, and support staff in implementing effective strategies for academic and social inclusion.

- Explore ways to empower children with Down syndrome to become active participants in their education, fostering self-confidence, self-advocacy, and a sense of belonging within the school community.

3. How does recognizing the potential for individuals with Down syndrome to lead fulfilling and independent lives as adults influence your perspective on the

importance of education as a foundation for future success and inclusion in society?

____

____

____

____

____

____

____

____

____

Points to ponder:

- Reflect on the evolving opportunities for adults with Down syndrome to live semi-independently, engage in community activities, and participate in meaningful work opportunities.

- Consider the role of education in equipping individuals with Down syndrome with the skills, knowledge, and confidence to navigate adulthood and pursue their goals and aspirations.

- Explore the importance of promoting lifelong learning and continued growth for individuals with Down syndrome, emphasizing the value of education as a pathway to empowerment, self-expression, and social integration.

Are there are some tips or criteria in choosing the right school for a child with Down syndrome?

Selecting the best school for a child with Down syndrome is a big choice that requires careful consideration.

It has both challenging and rewarding to navigate the educational landscape as a parent of a child with Down syndrome. Nicole's path to choose the best school for her has involved careful consideration and heartfelt decisions. Even though it hasn't been simple, I really think that finding a school that truly caters to her needs is paramount.

A good school for a child with Down syndrome, in my opinion, is one that values diversity and exhibits a deep understanding of each child's individual journey.

As parents, we have the responsibility to advocate for our children's educational needs. This occasionally entails looking for special schools that can meet their unique needs when mainstream options fall short. Despite her academic struggles, Nicole was fortunate enough to be able to attend a regular school. It has been immensely satisfying to see her excitement for learning and the happiness she finds in her teachers and classmates.

Nicole's teacher's persistent support and dedication made her experience in a mainstream school possible. We are incredibly appreciative of her kindness, tolerance, and sincere love for Nicole, all of which have surely aided in her development and   enjoyment   in   the   classroom.

As parents of children with Down syndrome, we found comfort in selecting a school that aligned with our family's values and preferences. Every choice we make, whether it's where preschool peers are likely to enroll or whether to prioritize proximity over a school where older siblings attend, is done so with our child's best interests in mind.

It's heartening to know that children with Down syndrome can be included in both public and private schools with relative ease. Many institutions are open to collaboration and eager to exchange knowledge and techniques to better support their students. Children like Nicole may flourish in their educational journeys and pave the path for a brighter future full of limitless possibilities with the help of this network of understanding and support.

Ultimately, the ideal educational institution for kids with Down syndrome is one that makes them feel accepted, encouraged, and equipped to realize their greatest potential.

Guide Questions for Self- Reflection:

1. How does understanding the importance of diversity, inclusivity, and a supportive environment in school settings influence your criteria for selecting the right school for a child with Down syndrome?

____

____

____

____

____

____

____

____

____

____

____

Points to ponder:

- Reflect on the significance of choosing a school that values and celebrates diversity, fostering an inclusive environment where all students, including those with Down syndrome, feel welcomed and supported.

- Consider how a school's understanding of children's individual needs and abilities can contribute to creating a positive and nurturing learning environment for students with Down syndrome.

- Explore the role of school culture and ethos in promoting acceptance, respect, and collaboration among students, staff, and families, enhancing the overall educational experience for children with Down syndrome.

2. How can parents navigate the decision-making process when choosing between mainstream and special schools for their child with Down syndrome, considering factors such as the child's individual needs, preferences, and potential for inclusion?

____

____

____

____

____

____

____

____

____

____

Points to ponder:

- Reflect on the importance of considering the specific needs and abilities of your child with Down syndrome when evaluating different school options, including mainstream and special schools.

- Consider how factors such as access to support services, inclusive practices, and opportunities for socialization and peer interaction may differ between mainstream and special schools, and how these factors align with your child's educational and developmental goals.

- Explore strategies for collaborating with educators, therapists, and other professionals to make informed decisions about the most suitable school environment for your child, taking into account their unique strengths, challenges, and learning style.

3. How does understanding the rights and options available to parents, such as the right to request a special school or access additional support services, empower you to advocate for your child's educational needs and preferences?

____

____

____

____

____

____

____

____

____

Points to ponder:

- Reflect on the importance of knowing your rights as a parent and advocating for your child's educational rights and needs within the school system.

- Consider how factors such as parental choice, access to resources, and collaboration with school personnel can influence the quality of education and support services available to children with Down syndrome.

- Explore strategies for effectively communicating with school administrators, teachers, and support staff to ensure that your child's educational experience is tailored to their individual needs, preferences, and aspirations.

What special educational needs will a child with Down syndrome have?

In order to ensure their success in the classroom, children with Down syndrome may have a variety of special educational needs that call for specialized help. These needs frequently include cognitive delays, difficulties with fine and gross motor abilities, and difficulties with speech and language development. Additionally, in order to support their comprehension of concepts and full participation in academic activities, children with Down syndrome may benefit from individualized learning strategies and accommodations.

According to the *Good Schools Guide (n.d.)*, while there is a wide variance in the abilities of children with Down syndrome, the majority typically fall into the mild to moderate learning disability category.

Including children with Down Syndrome in mainstream schools

It's possible that your child is the first with Down syndrome the school has worked with in a long time, in which case certain modifications will be necessary to recognize and work with a child who might have more severe learning challenges than they have worked with in the past.

Schools that prioritize inclusiveness and are friendly will acknowledge these difficulties for what they are and prioritize your child's needs as a child.

A good school will:

- heed the worries expressed by parents;

• look for outside data on the educational demands and

other requirements of kids with Down syndrome from

reputable sources;

• consider it your child's right to be included;

- will be there for them during their entire time in school, not just as a temporary social experiment;

• aim to provide access to a well-rounded and expansive curriculum;
• use your imagination to come up with inventive methods to involve your child in every aspect of school life.

Guide Questions for Self- Reflection:

1. How does understanding the range of abilities and learning challenges associated with Down syndrome influence your approach to identifying and addressing your child's special educational needs within a mainstream school setting?

____

____

____

____

____

____

____

____

____

____

Points to ponder:

- Reflect on the importance of recognizing the individual strengths and limitations of children with Down syndrome, considering factors such as processing speed and the need for additional practice in learning new skills.

- Consider how instructional strategies that incorporate both linguistic and visual cues can support your child's learning and participation in the classroom.

- Explore ways to collaborate with educators and school personnel to create a supportive and inclusive learning environment that accommodates your child's unique needs and promotes their academic and social development.

2. How can parents advocate for their child's educational needs within a mainstream school environment, ensuring that the school prioritizes inclusiveness and recognizes the challenges faced by children with Down syndrome?

____

____

____

____

____

____

____

____

____

____

____

Points to ponder:

- Reflect on the importance of voicing concerns and advocating for appropriate accommodations and support services that address your child's special educational needs.

- Consider the role of collaboration between parents, educators, and school administrators in identifying and implementing effective strategies for supporting children with Down syndrome in mainstream classrooms.

- Explore ways to gather outside data and resources from reputable sources to inform the school's understanding of the educational demands and requirements of children with Down syndrome, promoting a more informed and inclusive approach to supporting diverse learners.

3. How can parents work with schools to ensure that their child with Down syndrome receives a comprehensive and inclusive education that honors their individual accomplishments and fosters their full participation in school life?

Points to ponder:

- Reflect on the importance of building positive relationships with school personnel, fostering open communication, and advocating for your child's right to be included and supported throughout their educational journey.

- Consider the role of schools in providing access to a well-rounded and expansive curriculum that accommodates the diverse needs and interests of all students, including those with Down syndrome.

- Explore creative and innovative ways to involve your child in every aspect of school life, promoting their social integration, self-esteem, and overall well-being within the school community.

Do parents of a child with Down syndrome have any advice for parents new to this situation?

As a parent of a child with Down Syndrome, allow me to share some pieces of advice for those who are just starting out on this journey. Truly, we must seek assistance and make connections with other families who are aware of the challenges and joys associated with parenting a child with Down Syndrome. We must focus on our child's strengths and celebrate every milestone, no matter how small.

It is also preferable if we make sure our kids have access to the resources, care, and support they need for their development and well-being.

Finally, we have to accept our special children for who they are, understanding that the most effective strategies for navigating this one-of-a-kind and fulfilling journey are unconditional love, patience, and acceptance.

Here are some valuable pieces of advice for parents raising a child with Down syndrome, compiled from insights shared by Care.com (2024) and from interviews with experienced parents who have firsthand

knowledge of navigating the challenges and joys of raising children with Down syndrome.

• Treat your child with the same respect as any other. Prioritize the fact that your child is here, followed by their unique needs.

• Down syndrome kids are frequently happy and loving. Take a lesson on enjoying life from them.

• Never undervalue the potential of your child. You could be astonished if you don't have any upper bounds.

• Engage your child in play.

• As soon as you can, get therapy—speech, occupational, physical, and educational.

• As much as you can, include your child in the community.

• If your pediatrician advises that your child see a specialist, follow through.

• Give your child positive experiences in a variety of settings and with a wide range of individuals.

• Call your child by name frequently, particularly while praising them.

• Take advantage of the opportunity to learn as much as you can from experts who visit your home to work with your child. Find out about more useful resources and how you might push your child with some of the activities they perform.

• Establish a space that is appropriate for your child's needs and skills. Promote ambulation and discovery.

• Let your kids play with toys that vary in size and texture.

• Recognize that your child will grow in her own time and manner.

• Recognize that it can take several attempts to get her to perform a task correctly.

Remember:

• In schools, children with Down syndrome typically require extra assistance or attention.

- Children and infants diagnosed with Down syndrome frequently benefit from interventions aimed at enhancing their physical and mental disabilities. Among these are occupational treatment, speech therapy, and physical coordination exercises.

- Each newborn with Down syndrome is unique.

Guide Questions for Self- Reflection:

1. How can parents new to the experience of raising a child with Down syndrome prioritize their child's unique needs while also treating them with the same respect and dignity as any other child?

____

____

____

____

____

Points to ponder:

- Reflect on the importance of embracing your child's individuality and celebrating their strengths and abilities, while also recognizing and addressing their specific needs and challenges.

- Consider how adopting a mindset of respect and acceptance can foster a positive and nurturing environment for your child's growth and development.

- Explore strategies for advocating for your child's rights and inclusion within the family, community, and educational settings, while also promoting their autonomy and self-esteem.

2. How can parents draw inspiration from the joyful and loving nature of children with Down syndrome, incorporating lessons on enjoying life and finding happiness in everyday moments?

____

____

____

____

____

____

____

____

____

____

Points to ponder:

- Reflect on the resilience and optimism displayed by many children with Down syndrome, and how their joyful approach to life can serve as a source of inspiration for parents facing challenges.

- Consider how fostering a sense of joy, playfulness, and positivity within the family can enhance the overall well-being and quality of life for both parents and their child with Down syndrome.

- Explore strategies for incorporating moments of play, laughter, and connection into daily routines, prioritizing experiences that bring joy and fulfillment to both parent and child.

3. How can parents advocate for their child's educational and developmental needs, ensuring access to appropriate therapies, interventions, and support services while also promoting their child's inclusion and participation in the community?

____

____

____

____

____

____

____

____

____

____

Points to ponder:

- Reflect on the importance of actively engaging in your child's educational journey, advocating for their rights and access to quality services and support.

- Consider the significance of monitoring your child's progress and ensuring that their Individualized Educational Program (IEP) is being implemented effectively, advocating for adjustments and accommodations as needed.

- Explore strategies for promoting your child's participation in community activities and fostering meaningful connections with peers and caregivers, while also providing opportunities for growth, learning, and socialization.

As Nicole's story draws to an end, I'm reminded of the important lessons her journey has taught us. I give this advice to all the parents navigating the joys and challenges of having kids with Down syndrome: savor every second, treasure every accomplishment, and cling steadfastly to hope. Nicole's resilience has taught us that love has no boundaries and that our kids can achieve extraordinary things if we give them the patience, empathy, and unwavering support they need. May Nicole's story be a beacon of hope, showing us the way forward with courage, grace, and unending love.

Remember, dear parents, you are not alone, embrace the journey, the successes, and the beauty that may be found in every step along the way. May God bless us all.

References/Sources

Global Down Syndrome Foundation (2024). *Facts and FAQ about Down syndrome.* https://www.globaldownsyndrome.org/abo ut-down-syndrome/facts-about-down-syndrome/#Whatis

Care.com. (2024). *Caring for a child with Down syndrome.* https://www.care.com/special-needs-caring-for-a-child-with-down-syndrome- p1167-q16876.html

N.P. Hamilton (2022) *Down Syndrome.* https://kidshealth.org/en/parents/down-syndrome.html

The Good Schools Guide (n.d.) *Difficulties children with Down's syndrome experience.* http://www.goodschoolsguide.co.uk/help-and- advice/special-needs-advice/types of-sen/genetic-disorders/187/down-s-syndrome

Special Thanks:

Down Syndrome Association of the Philippines, Inc. (DSAPI), *for providing a platform for parents of children with Down Syndrome to connect, bond, and share their experiences.*

AUTHOR'S PROFILE

Dr. Simplicio Pangilinan Alba, *a licensed professional teacher and civil service professional licensee, has been in the teaching field for the past thirty-two years now. His previous experiences as a classroom teacher, coordinator, researcher, editor, internal quality auditor, director, principal, dean, speaker and facilitator in seminar-workshops for teachers and students exposed him to fruitful learnings about the many "know-hows" of the teaching profession including school leadership management.*

He is the author and coordinator of nine books published by C and E Publishing House, Inc. titled "Smart Connections: Worktext in English" and "Learn English the Smart Ways (Series)" for Basic Education; the guest author of the book "Reflective Leadership and Management in Action" published by EduHeart Book Publishing; likewise, the author of "Brushstrokes of Wisdom" published by Poetry Planet Publishing House.

Beyond his academic and professional accomplishments, he exemplifies love and devotion as a husband to Rhea and a father to their two children, Engr. Joshua and Nicole, who has Down Syndrome.